WOMEN
LEADING
THE WAY

Zaha Hadid
Architect

by Christina Leaf

BLASTOFF! READERS
2

BELLWETHER MEDIA • MINNEAPOLIS, MN

Note to Librarians, Teachers, and Parents:

Blastoff! Readers are carefully developed by literacy experts and combine standards-based content with developmentally appropriate text.

Level 1 provides the most support through repetition of high-frequency words, light text, predictable sentence patterns, and strong visual support.

Level 2 offers early readers a bit more challenge through varied simple sentences, increased text load, and less repetition of high-frequency words.

Level 3 advances early-fluent readers toward fluency through increased text and concept load, less reliance on visuals, longer sentences, and more literary language.

Level 4 builds reading stamina by providing more text per page, increased use of punctuation, greater variation in sentence patterns, and increasingly challenging vocabulary.

Level 5 encourages children to move from "learning to read" to "reading to learn" by providing even more text, varied writing styles, and less familiar topics.

Whichever book is right for your reader, Blastoff! Readers are the perfect books to build confidence and encourage a love of reading that will last a lifetime!

This edition first published in 2019 by Bellwether Media, Inc.

No part of this publication may be reproduced in whole or in part without written permission of the publisher. For information regarding permission, write to Bellwether Media, Inc., Attention: Permissions Department, 6012 Blue Circle Drive, Minnetonka, MN 55343.

Library of Congress Cataloging-in-Publication Data

Names: Leaf, Christina, author.
Title: Zaha Hadid : Architect / by Christina Leaf.
Description: Minneapolis, MN : Bellwether Media, Inc., 2019. | Series: Blastoff! Readers: Women Leading the Way | Includes bibliographical references and index. | Audience: Ages 5-8. | Audience: K to Grade 3
Identifiers: LCCN 2018033936 (print) | LCCN 2018034671 (ebook) | ISBN 9781681036700 (ebook) | ISBN 9781626179462 (hardcover : alk. paper) | ISBN 9781618915078 (pbk. : alk. paper)
Subjects: LCSH: Hadid, Zaha–Juvenile literature. | Architects–Iraq–Biography–Juvenile literature. | Women architects-Iraq–Biography–Juvenile literature.
Classification: LCC NA1469.H33 (ebook) | LCC NA1469.H33 L43 2019 (print) | DDC 720.92 [B] –dc23
LC record available at https://lccn.loc.gov/2018033936

Editor: Kate Moening   Designer: Andrea Schneider

Printed in the United States of America, North Mankato, MN.

Table of Contents

Who Was Zaha Hadid?

Dame Zaha Hadid was a famous **architect**. Her imaginative buildings stand across the world.

They earned her the nickname, "Queen of the Curve."

Heydar Aliyev Center Museum (Azerbaijan, 2013)

"I WILL NEVER GIVE MYSELF THE LUXURY OF THINKING 'I'VE MADE IT.' ... I ALWAYS SET THE BAR HIGHER."
(2013)

Zaha was born in Baghdad, Iraq, in 1950. The city boomed with modern **design**.

Zaha Hadid Profile

Birthday: October 31, 1950

Hometown: Baghdad, Iraq

Industry: architecture

Education:
- math degree (American University in Beirut, Lebanon)
- architecture degree (Architectural Association in London, UK)

Influences and Heroes:
- Mohammed Hadid (Zaha's father)
- Rem Koolhaas (architect; Zaha's teacher)
- Kazimir Malevich (Russian artist)
- Oscar Niemeyer (architect)

Zaha knew architecture was her future **career** by age 11.

Getting Her Start

Zaha in her
London office

In 1972, Zaha moved to London to study architecture. After school, she started her own **firm**.

In 1983, she **bid** for a building design in Hong Kong. She won!

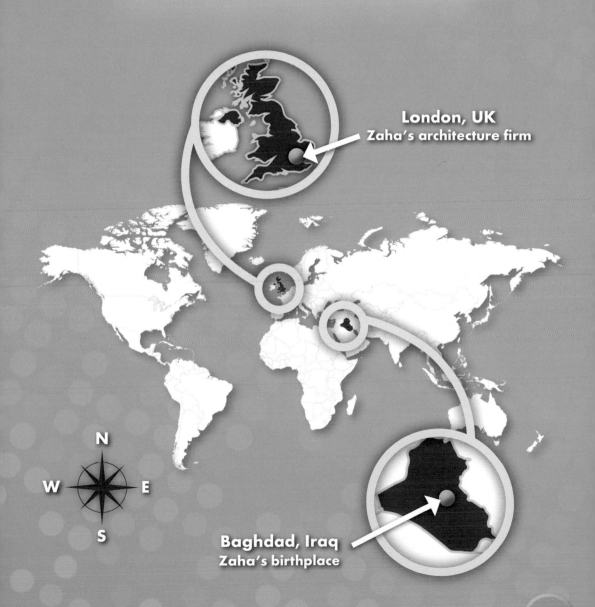

London, UK
Zaha's architecture firm

Baghdad, Iraq
Zaha's birthplace

N
W   E
S

People loved Zaha's design. But some thought it was **impractical**. It was never built.

Other designs also struggled. Zaha's first building was finally completed in 1993.

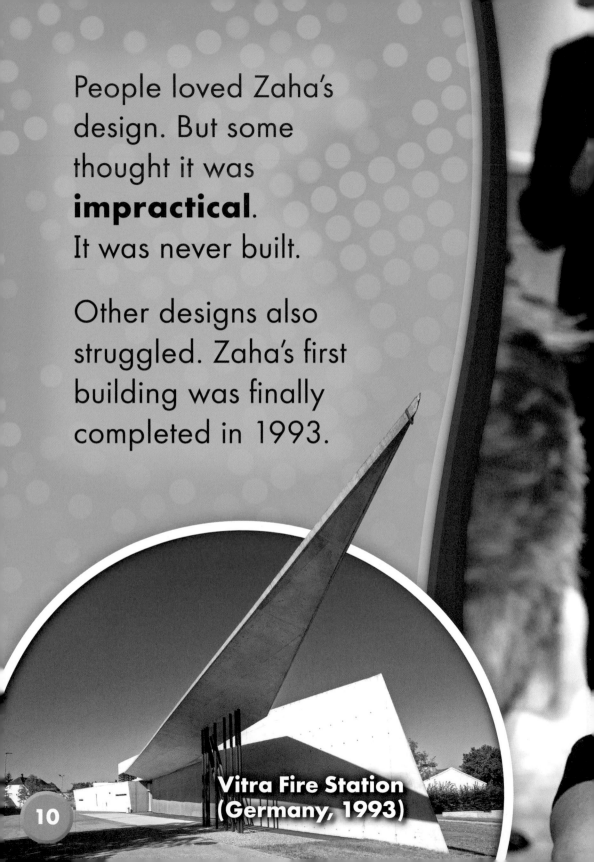

Vitra Fire Station (Germany, 1993)

Contemporary Arts Center
(Cincinnati, Ohio, 2003)

Later projects earned Zaha fame.
She was the first woman to
design an American museum.

Her Olympic **venue** in London wowed the world.

London Aquatics Centre (2011)

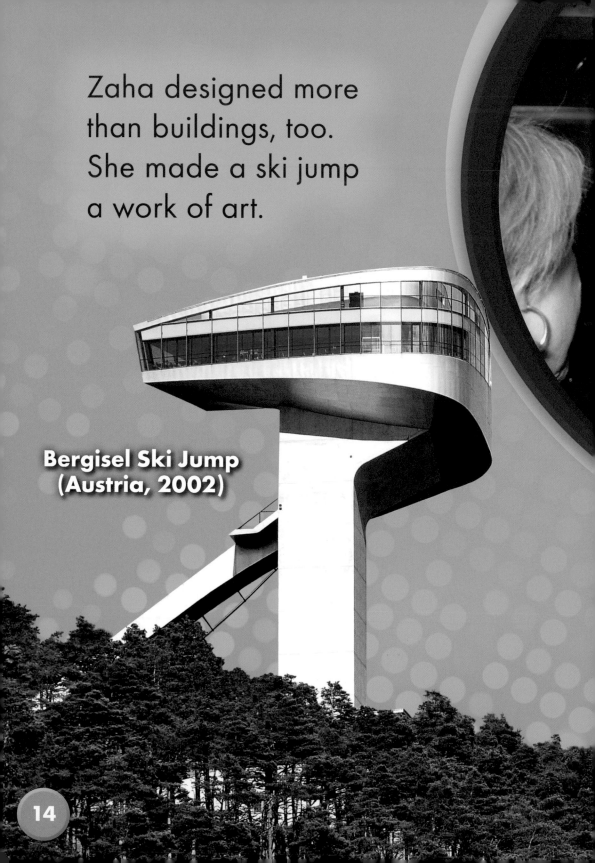

Zaha designed more than buildings, too. She made a ski jump a work of art.

Bergisel Ski Jump (Austria, 2002)

14

Other designs included
tables, bridges, and shoes!

It was difficult to be a woman in architecture. Most architects are men.

But many people thought Zaha was brilliant. Zaha was tough. She fought for respect.

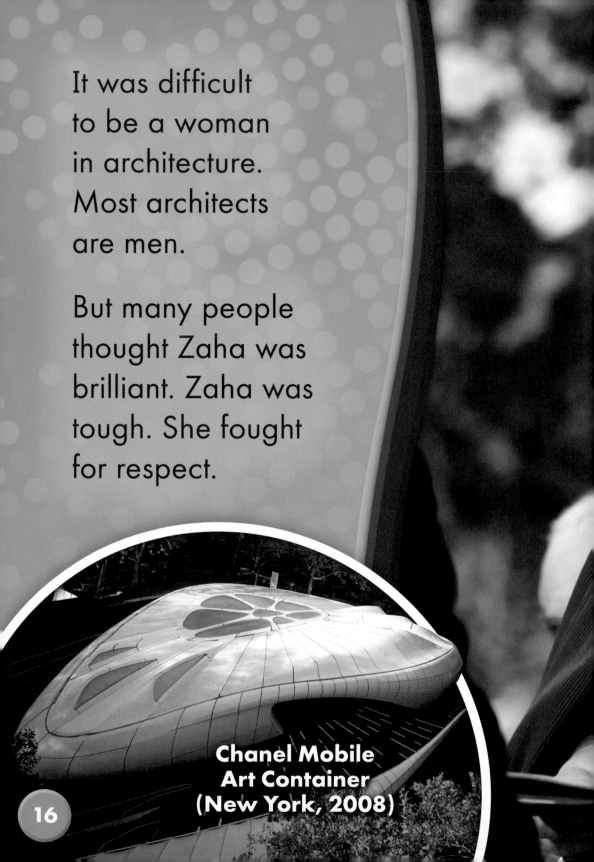

Chanel Mobile Art Container (New York, 2008)

"NEVER IN MY
UPBRINGING WAS
THERE A FEELING
THAT WOMEN
ARE DIFFERENT
FROM MEN."
(2008)

Zaha's work won many **awards**. Zaha was the first woman to receive the **Pritzker**.

Zaha Hadid Timeline

1950   Zaha is born in Baghdad, Iraq

1983   Zaha wins a design competition for a building in Hong Kong

1993   Zaha's first building is completed, a fire station in Germany

2004   Zaha is the first woman to win the Pritzker Architecture Prize

2016   Zaha passes away on March 31 in Miami, Florida

Later, she earned Britain's highest honor. The queen made her a dame!

Zaha's death in 2016 saddened many people. But her **inspiring** buildings still stand.

Her work opened doors for others to build their dreams!

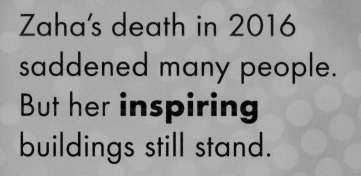

Dominion Tower
(Russia, 2015)

"ARCHITECTURE IS NO LONGER A MAN'S WORLD. THIS IDEA THAT WOMEN CAN'T THINK THREE DIMENSIONALLY IS RIDICULOUS." (2008)

Glossary

architect—a person who designs and plans buildings

awards—rewards or prizes that are given for a job well done

bid—attempted to win a project by entering a contest

career—a job someone does for a long time

dame—a woman who has reached knighthood; knighthood is the highest honor for a British citizen to receive.

design—a plan for a building, object, or pattern

firm—a company

impractical—more difficult than is useful

inspiring—giving an idea of what to do or create

Pritzker—an important architecture award

venue—a place where specific types of events happen

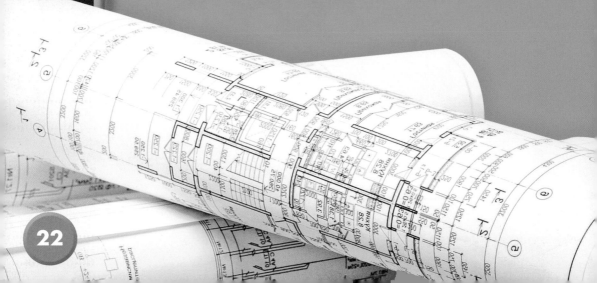

To Learn More

AT THE LIBRARY

Harvey, Jeanne Walker. *Maya Lin: Artist-Architect of Light and Lines*. New York, N.Y.: Henry Holt and Company, 2017.

Verhille, Alexandre, and Sarah Tavernier. *The Illustrated Atlas of Architecture and Marvelous Monuments*. New York, N.Y.: Little Gestalten, 2016.

Winter, Jeanette. *The World Is Not a Rectangle: A Portrait of Architect Zaha Hadid*. New York, N.Y.: Beach Lane Books, 2017.

ON THE WEB

FACTSURFER

Factsurfer.com gives you a safe, fun way to find more information.

1. Go to www.factsurfer.com.

2. Enter "Zaha Hadid" into the search box.

3. Click the "Surf" button and select your book cover to see a list of related web sites.

Index